When Lawyers Wept

When Lawyers Wept

Elizabeth S. Wolf

Cover design by Shay Culligan:

ISBN: 978-1-950462-24-7

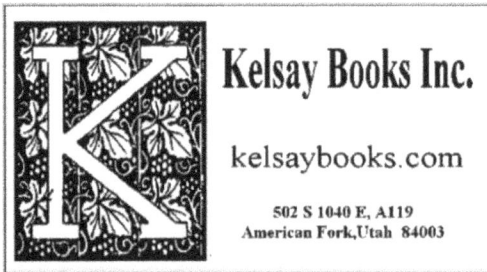

Kelsay Books Inc.

kelsaybooks.com

502 S 1040 E, A119
American Fork, Utah 84003

To the friends who became family,
along the long strange trip;
To all the dogs along the way;
And especially to my daughter Samantha,
who makes me proud, joyous, and most grateful.

Acknowledgments

National Poetry Journal: "to Norman" and "Night clouds."

Merrimac Mic Anthology: Gleanings from the First Year: "Borderlines," "The Minister's Wife"

Mosaics: A Collection of Independent Women: "Borderlines," "The Minister's Wife"

New Verse News: "Dangerous Women"

Peregrine: "Yes Sir"

Scarlet Leaf Review: "Germanwings 9525," "Grateful for Good Neighbors," "Every Addict is Somebody's Child"

What I Learned: Poems from Finishing Line Press, October 2017 "Borderlines," "Yes Sir," "The Minister's Wife," "Night clouds," "Revelation," "to Norman," "Character Study #1," "for Ben," "Germanwings 9525," "Grateful for Good Neighbors," "Off the Trail," and "Every Addict is Somebody's Child" are included in the chapbook

Merrimac Mic IV: Watershed: "Tangled Web," "It's the 10th anniversary"

Tuck Magazine: "The Busboy from the Ambassador Motel"

Ibbetson Street: "Between My Fingers Like a Shield"

Merrimac Mic Takes the Fifth: "I raised my hand," "Meeting the Host Family," "Primate Customs"

Did You Know? Summer 2019, Rattle Chapbook Contest 2018 Winner. "Tangled Web," "May 4, 1970", "The Center Did Not Hold," "August 8,1974," "Fall & Winter 1974," "July 23, 1975," "August 1975," "Summer: 1981," "Before She Knew," "August 1983," "The Wall Comes Tumbling Down," "That Night My Mother Called Me," "The Next Night My Mother Called," "The Following Night My Mother Called," "My Mother Called Again," "October 1983," "There Used to be Rules," "Circa 1986," "May 1986," "After She Knew," "July 1993," "March 1997," "April 2004," "Also April 2004," "April 2005," "April 2007," "Recycling the Travel Section," and "And in the end..."

The quote from "March 2004" is from *Millions of Cats*, written and illustrated by Wanda Gág. Coward-McCann, 1929.

Contents

Tangled Web   13
May 4, 1970   16
The Center Did Not Hold   18
August 8, 1974   20
Fall & Winter 1974   21
July 23, 1975   23
August 1975   24
Summer 1981   25
Before She Knew   26
August 1983   27
The Wall Comes Tumbling Down   28
That Night My Mother Called Me   29
The Next Night My Mother Called   30
The Following Night My Mother Called   31
My Mother Called Again   33
October 1983   34
There Used to be Rules   36
Circa 1986   38
May 1986   39
After She Knew   40
July 1993   41
March 1997   43
March 2004   44
April 2004   45
Also April 2004   46
April 2005   47
April 2007   48
Recycling the Travel section   50
And in the end...   51
The Road of Life   53
Goodbye Dogwood Tree   54
Goodbye Besties   56
Nightmare House   58
Goodbye Grade School   59

Yes Sir   61
The Minister's Wife   62
Borderlines   63
Free Range   64
Goodbye My First Love   66
Revelation   68
Night clouds.   69
to Norman   70
Character Study #1   71
Goodbye Marriage   75
Mourning the Living   78
Goodbye Ben   79
It's the 10th anniversary   81
Grateful for Good Neighbors   82
The Busboy from the Ambassador Hotel   83
Off the Trail   84
Germanwings 9525   85
Every Addict is Somebody's Child   91
Dangerous Women   94
Between My Fingers Like A Shield   98
Sisters on the Runway   100
I raised my hand   103
Touring in the People's Republic of China   104
Meeting the Host Family   108
Primate Customs   109

Did You Know?

Oh, what a tangled web we weave
When first we practice to deceive!
—Walter Scott, *Marmion: A Tale of Flodden Field*

Tangled Web

Before HIPAA
      before women could carry credit cards in their own names
      back when discussing birth control with unmarried women
            could land you in the Charles Street Jail—
my mother's legs were tingling. Some days they felt
hot, swollen, and stiff; some days they didn't feel
much at all. My mother spent summer afternoons
sitting on her screened-in porch with bags of frozen vegetables
draped over her legs, needlepoint in hand, or a deck of cards
for a wicked game of bridge.

One fall my mother went blind in one eye.
But then her vision returned.

My father was a lawyer. We had
the best of Boston health care.
When my mother's primary care physician
and her consulting neurologist
and her ophthalmologist
concluded the most likely diagnosis
was multiple sclerosis,
they let my father know
over lunch, with drinks,
in town at the club.

My father was a first-generation
American, a bombardier in
World War II, a graduate of Harvard
back when there were quotas for Jews.
My father was the dictionary definition of
responsibility and competence.

My father was lost.

He sought counsel of his best friend, RM,
a fellow lawyer.

He sought counsel of his best friend, Dr. K.,
now their physician.

He went before his formidable father-in-law
who had founded the law firm my father now managed.

Late in the fall of 1968
        after bullets felled Martin and Bobby
        after the Tet Offensive and the
                Broadway opening of *Hair*
my father, filled with the best of
intentions, made an awful decision:
to keep my mother's diagnosis
a secret. From her.

Believing the stress of naming the disease
would make it worse, my father chose
to be her guardian, the gatekeeper
of incoming information. He would tell her
when the time was right. He was certain
he would know
when the time was right.

This was something he could do. He could protect
my mother. From her own body. He accepted that burden
as a husband's duty.

So my father signed up
her primary care physician
her consulting neurologist
her ophthalmologist

her father and her mother
many friends and cousins

and swore them to secrecy.

My father managed this whole conspiracy
flawlessly. Until the summer of 1975, when he unexpectedly
dropped dead. He was 50. His widow was 45.
His children were 22, 19, and 16.

My father left an insurance policy and an estate plan.
My father left no instructions for how to handle the secret.
And so
         it continued to be kept.

May 4, 1970

When the National Guard killed four students at Kent State,
injuring nine more, my father was wounded. The dead looked
like his children. The National Guard looked like his children.
His government was shooting unarmed citizens. It was not
what his family came to America for. It was not what my father
fought for, trained for, decades before, flying missions over
Germany, upholding the oath of a bombardier before he was
old enough to vote. It was not right. He was not right.

For years, arguing with my brothers, my father had declared:
"When your country calls, you go." And, "My country, right
or wrong." What if it was wrong?

My parents had a big house in the suburbs, good schools,
a green lawn, a fenced yard. My brother's friends gathered
on the porch and talked about the war, about Nixon,
about the draft, about the bombs, about the lies.
Were the soldiers in My Lai only following orders?
Where had we heard that before?

My father locked the door between the porch and the
dining room; he opened the window between the porch
and the kitchen and passed out the black rotary dial phone.
He closed the window but for a thin crack for the cord.
The boys on the porch became the local
Kent State Strike Committee.

We skipped school. I learned to run a Gestetner mimeo machine,
making copies of leaflets to staple on telephone poles around town.
We organized sit-ins and marches; we shared food and clothes.
Sometimes I walked out the porch door and into the main house.

I did loads of laundry in the basement. I made sandwiches
and cookies. I walked out the kitchen door
and back into the porch. I was 11.

My father used to say there was nothing a girl could do
worth paying for. Girl talk was vapid. Back talk was verboten.

I was a ready recruit for the war at home.

The Center Did Not Hold

My oldest brother went to college
in the fall of 1970. For Thanksgiving that year,
my father flew my middle brother to visit on campus.
My father made vacation plans with my mother.
He told me, you can do whatever you want
for Thanksgiving, as long as it isn't with us.
            I was 12.

I went to stay with a friend. I did that
more and more. I was the kid who came for dinner
and stayed three days.

The next Thanksgiving, my friend's parents
starting bickering after the guests were gone.
What is wrong with this child? asked her mother.
It is Thanksgiving, and no one in her family
will speak to her.

I didn't stay there any more holidays.

I walked into the local multiservice center and
said I needed a place to live.
And so began
            the revolving gyre
                        that lasted the rest of my childhood.

My father was fine to see me go. But
he refused to surrender custody.

In Massachusetts in the 1970's
anyone who housed a minor child
for three months could sue
for physical custody.

And so
        at least every ninety days
        (and sometimes more often)
                I moved.

Sometimes I was in foster care.
Sometimes I ran away.
Sometimes I stayed with friends.
Sometimes I ran away.
Sometimes I worked for room and board.
Sometimes I ran away.
Sometimes I went back to the land
with a cousin doing subsistence farming
but I couldn't go to school without
  a custodial adult.
And so the cycle repeated.

I was sent to boarding school.
I ran away.
I was expelled from boarding school.
And so the cycle repeated.

My father died. And still,
the cycle repeated. There was an even
higher law in play: A body in motion
tends to remain in motion.

August 8, 1974

My parents got a color television
after men walked on the moon.
Richard Nixon always appeared
a bilious shade of yellow-green.
"Don't adjust the set," my mother would say.
"That's just him." My father, Mr. Republican,
would object. My mother kept working
on her needlepoint.

The August that Nixon resigned, I was
at a friend's in Deering, New Hampshire.
Their summer retreat had no phone and no
television. We walked down the dirt road,
to the home Lotte Jacobi shared with
Beatrice Trum Hunter. Lotte was a famous
photographer: she took portraits of
Einstein, Chagall, Eleanor Roosevelt. Bea was
a natural foods maven: she provided
pesticide research to Rachael Carson for
"Silent Spring." I did not know this then.
Lotte and Bea were neighbors; Lotte took pictures
of my friends searching for turtles or playing with
Breyer plastic horses. Watching that
historic speech with those incredible women,
I was thinking about
                          arguing with my father,
if he would yell, if we would ever talk again. I was
a fierce rebel, completely unaware of the blinders
still solidly soldered to my eyes. I didn't know
women could be heroes.

Fall & Winter 1974

For my junior year, I was sent away to
prep school. Two hours west, with lots of
rules and a lovely chapel. School and
boarding combined. Problem solved.

In October I got sick.
I went to the infirmary but they said
I was seeking attention, and sent me away.

Two hours later I was back.
My temperature was over 103.
They let me stay.

My fever spiked, and my joints swelled
and ached. Finally the school doctor
called my father. "We are taking her to the
hospital tomorrow," the doctor said.
"They will most likely admit her."

"Boston is the medical mecca of the world,"
my father said. "If my daughter needs to be
in a hospital, she needs to be in Boston."

My father had a very important client meeting.
So they arranged for my mother to fetch me the
following day. The doctor called back later.
"Put a mattress in the back of the car," he suggested.
"Your daughter can't sit up for that long a ride."

My mother drove out with a friend. Someone helped me
to the mattress. We drove east. My mother pulled the car
into the driveway and locked it. I was in the back,
in and out of sleep.

My mother called my father. "I can't handle this," she said.
"It's too much for me. You have to come home now."

So my father left his very important client and drove
to the suburbs. My mother stayed inside the house.
I stayed locked in the car, in and out of sleep.

By the time we reached the ER
I was running 105 and delirious.

I spent three weeks inpatient with rheumatic fever. I could have
been discharged earlier but no one would take me home. I went
back to school with polyarthritis lingering in my wrists and ankles.
I spent Thanksgiving in the dorm, catching up on schoolwork.

In January the school had an intersession. I had signed up for
Spanish guitar and cross-country skiing. I could do neither.
The school refused to let me switch classes. The time period
for changing classes was closed.

"But I was in the hospital," I said.
"We have rules," said the dean.

Neither teacher wanted me present but benched.
"It disrupts the class," they said.
"We have rules," said the dean.

So the teachers told me not to show up
and not to get caught. Every morning I left the dorm
before 8 a.m. I did not return until after 4.

It was a cold and snowy winter
filled with structure and lacking any mercy.

July 23, 1975

My mother and father were at a golf course
on a sunny summer Wednesday afternoon. First tee.
My mother turned to watch my father's drive.
It never came. He lay on the ground at her feet.

After the ambulance, the ER, and gathering
my brothers, my mother called my school.
I was working as a mother's helper and taking
summer classes. That night we were on a field trip
to see *King Lear,* in Connecticut. Rather than
intercepting the bus and making me wait
at a state police station, they decided
to send my brothers to pick up after the show.

I don't remember the play at all. I was restless
all night. Something, somewhere, was very
very wrong. The drama teacher scolded me
all the way back. When I saw two guys waiting
on the walkway, I leapt out of the van. I thought
it was time to party. When my brothers told me
what had happened, I didn't believe.

We drove south on Route 91 by the Connecticut River,
then the Mass Pike east towards Boston. My
mother was sleeping on her screened porch while
family friends waited for us. Just after 2 a.m. my mother
woke up and went to the back door. "My children
are here," she said, as we pulled into the driveway.

August 1975

After summer school ended,
I went to my mother's. I thought maybe
I could go home.

Two days later my mother stood in the doorway
of what was once my room. "My friend J is coming
to visit," she said. "I thought I'd put her in here."

"OK," I said. My mother stumbled as she turned
and wall-walked down the hall.

I left the next day. I stayed with friends
until the dorms re-opened in the fall.

Summer 1981

My grandfather used to gather his family
and close friends for milestone birthdays.
He would fly his daughters and their
families to a resort location and
ensconce them all in a fine hotel.

Except for me.

In 1981 he flew in my brother from California
and my cousin from Texas. I was in Arizona.
Too far, he declared.

I was hurt and angry.
I asked my mother and brothers
to stand up for me. "It's his party,"
said my mother. "He can invite
whoever he wants."

"Why do you want to go?" asked my
middle brother. "We don't."

"So skip it," I suggested.

"Can't," he answered. "It is a
command performance."

Before She Knew

My mother shopped for groceries
at the oddest hours, when she was least likely
to see anyone she knew. My mother had a
wobbly gait and needed to clutch the cart.
It takes a lot of steps to get through a supermarket.
My mother was afraid her neighbors would gossip
that she was always drunk.

When my mother did drink,
she used a paper cup. The nice glasses
from the bar set kept slipping from her hands.

Sometimes my mother sat halfway up the stairs
and halfway down, like the Christopher Robin poem.
I found her there reading more than once. She was afraid
one day her legs would fail and she would be stranded
forever upstairs or down.

Sometimes after she sipped scotch from her paper cup
my mother crawled. She was afraid if she fell down
she might not be able to get back up.

My mother got tired and napped often.
It stressed her out. My mother recited
nursery rhymes to soothe her worried mind.

My mother feared she was going insane.
She didn't tell anyone.
Her children were embarrassed and didn't say a word.

August 1983

My oldest brother, married and with a
baby, was moving to L.A. My other brother
was already there. I lived south of Worcester.

A cousin took my brother to lunch.
"When you leave," said the cousin,
"your mother will have no children left
in the east."

I don't know if my brother mentioned
that I was still in Massachusetts.

"Before you go," said the cousin,
"you should know: your mother
is sick. She has M.S."

My brother was stunned. "She never said!"
he protested.

"She doesn't know," said the cousin.
"Someone has to tell her."

The Wall Comes Tumbling Down

My brother called Dr K.
and said: "It's over. You
have to tell my mother
all about multiple sclerosis
and that she has it.
I can't tell her.
I don't even know
what the hell it is.
You're a doctor.
You can answer questions."

"What about her parents?"
asked Dr K.

"They can't diagnose," said my brother.
"Take care of your patient first.
Then the rest of the players
can answer for their sins."

That Night My Mother Called Me

"Did you know?" she asked.
"Know what?" I responded.
"Did you know the secret?" she asked.
"What secret?" I responded.

Only my brothers, my mother and I
            and one true friend
had been unaware of her diagnosis.

Now there was an "us":
the ones who did not know.

And with that I was restored.

The Next Night My Mother Called

"I can't talk to my parents,"
she said. "I am so mad.
My mother came over with a hot lunch
and I didn't open the door."

"Good for you," I said. "You talk
to who you want,
when you want.
It's your house.
It's your life."

"Life sucks," said my mother.
 "Also true," I replied.

The Following Night My Mother Called

It was very late. She was whispering.
"Your father's friend RM and his new wife
are here," she said.

"What the heck?" I responded.
"It's midnight."

"They called and wanted to come over
and I said no!" said my mother. "They called
again. I didn't answer the phone."

"Ma," I said. "You talk to
who you want,
when you want.
It's your life. It's under
your control."

"But they came anyway", she whispered.
"They are knocking at the back door.
I'm hiding under the window upstairs
in the study with the phone."

"Ma," I said. "You don't have to hide."
"What do I do?" she whispered back.
"Is the alarm on?" I asked.
"Of course," she said. "I was in bed."
"Ma," I said. "Open the window."
"But the alarm—" she started.
"Exactly," I said.

My mother put down the receiver.

Within a minute I heard sirens
followed by car doors slamming.

My mother hung up to call off the police.

My Mother Called Again

"I need a ride," she said.
"No one will take me."

"I will," I said.
"Where do you want to go?"

"I want to go to Sharon," said my mother,
"and stomp on your father's grave."

"Go ahead," I said. "It won't
hurt him. You do whatever
you need to do."

"No one will take me there," she said.

"I will," I said again.

"You can't," said my mother.
"It's not something I can ask
my children to do."

"Sure you can," I said. "And if it helps
I won't watch."

"Thank you," she said. "But no."

October 1983

While my mother's life imploded
I was flat on my back. That fall my doctor,
physical therapist, and chiropractor all agreed
it was time for surgery. There were no robotics
or microsurgeries then. A neurosurgeon literally
held your nerves out of the way while an
orthopedic surgeon reshaped vertebrae.
It was a big deal.

I lived alone on a lake. This was no longer feasible.

A friend was willing to house me for the months of recovery,
at her apartment in Atlanta. I first had to stabilize from surgery
in Boston.

My mother offered to take me in. She moved a stretcher
into her living room. Until I was well enough to fly.

The first time I was alone in her home, the phone rang.
It was her cousin, the one famous for welcoming family.
Except for me.

Cousin said, "We don't think you should be at your mother's.
It's too much for her right now."

I said, "Oh! Your invitation must have gotten lost in the move.
I've barely unpacked. I can be ready in an hour, if you want
to pick me up and bring me back to your house."

The cousin spluttered and stammered.

I said, "Oh! You thought I had lots of options! I don't, really.
I am leaving as soon as I can. Until then, my mother
invited me to stay here. And I think right now is a
good time to let her decide what she can and cannot do."

There Used to be Rules

My mother told me once, when I was in my 30's,
she couldn't imagine how hard it must be to
have choices. In her day good girls were virgins at their
weddings, and that was that. And then the 60's
happened, and free love, and then in the 70's,
abortion was legal. Without the pregnancy card,
the whole game was changed.

My mother had rules for everything. Always
side with your husband. Be courteous
to the help. Tip the mailman and the paperboy
at Christmas. Towels are folded in thirds.
She knew what to wear and when; what to
serve for lunch or brunch or dinner; what to
wash in hot or cold. Her sheets were ironed.

I was visiting my mother in the mid-80's when
she stopped outside the bedroom door.

"What do you think?" she asked.
"About what?" I wondered.
"Did you see?" she asked.
I looked around the room.
 "Look at the bed," she said.
So I did.
"Look harder," she said.
So I did.
"I used the top sheet from one set
with a different fitted sheet," she declared.
"I thought you'd get a kick out of that."

I stared at the bed.

I stared at my mother.

She was positively delighted with her act of rebellion.

My mind reeled. How sheltered was she? What did she see
when she looked at me? Does she know how I lived as an
outcast, a foster child? Nights with no place to sleep, I crashed in
shelters, wards, hallways, under bushes, in
borrowed sleeping bags. I fucked friends
for a place to sleep.

But here I was, over 21, and she was wearing an ankle brace,
swaying on crutches to stay upright. The whole game
was changed.

I accepted her gift.

"Wow!" I answered. "I thought I woke up
extra spunky. Now I know why!"

She turned and crutched down the hall, giggling.

I stood staring at the space where my mother had been.

Circa 1986

For years after my father died
he was mailed the most amazing offers.
Life insurance, no physical required!
Credits cards, with low low interest!

Sometimes we considered cashing them in.
But at some point the scheme involved stealing.
So mostly the junk mail was recycled.

When Discover was launched, they mailed my father
a real deal. No annual fee. Sky-high credit limit.
My mother crossed out his name, wrote in hers,
and sent it back.

Two weeks later she was notified
her application was rejected.

Incensed, my mother called the 800 number on the letter.
"You offered credit to a dead man!" she exclaimed. "And then
refused a woman who has paid all of her bills for years!
That's sexist."

The operator promised the management would reconsider.

Two weeks later she was notified
her application was accepted.

My mother cut the card in half and mailed it back,
with a note. You made your most generous offer
to a man who has been dead for a decade. I wouldn't want
to patronize a company like yours. And she signed it,
Most Sincerely.

May 1986

After the secret came out,
I was included. But still
second rate. My grandfather
flew us all out to San Diego
and got hotel rooms for everyone.

Except for me.

I wasn't hurt or angry.
I was amused. I camped with my
brother and my cousins and raided
the hospitality fridge.

"Seems the great and powerful
'man behind the curtain' is afraid
of me!" I marveled. "Just what superpower
do I secretly possess?"

After She Knew

My mother did a lot of research.
She chose all new doctors. My mother
joined support groups and signed us
all up for newsletters.

My mother moved to accessible housing,
with mobility aids, within two years of the
conspiracy collapsing. My mother named her
crutches: Fuck and Shit.

My mother enrolled in a clinical trial.
They gave her chemo to knock out her
immune system. She lost her hair and
never walked again. She spent two months
in a rehab hospital. They spread lined sheets
over her bed and chair, in case of accidents.

My mother pinned the sheet to her
shoulders like a cape, threw off her
wig, and raced down the hallways
full tilt boogie in her cherry red Rascal.

My mother was a rocking superhero.

July 1993

When my grandfather died,
lawyers wept. The family
held a roast, presided over by his
younger daughter, at a hotel
by the funeral home,
probably on his dime.

It made me a little uneasy.
"It's just not right," I said.
My aunt said, "Let's have a
contest. Who did he say
the worst thing to? Who did he
treat the most badly?"
My grandfather hadn't spoken to me
in years. I went home.

The next morning over breakfast,
my aunt told me I was declared
the winner. "But I wasn't there,"
I said. "Exactly!" said my aunt. "You
were excommunicated, dear.
Shunned. Cast out."

I took a sip of coffee and waited.

"Did you know, when your father died—"
"When I was 16," I chimed in—
"Exactly. Well. Your grandfather, my father,
declared you were such a bad daughter,
it killed your father. And that's why
he so suddenly died."

I was stunned.
"Really?" I asked.

"Truly," she answered. "Neither man
thought you did enough
to take care of your mother."

"I was a child," I said. "And, I didn't know
that she needed to be taken care of."

My aunt reached for her purse.
"Did anyone ever tell you?" she asked.

"No. Not until this very moment," I replied.

My aunt poured a nip bottle of Grand Marnier
into her cereal bowl. "There," she said.
"You won."

March 1997

I got married at 38.
My mother was so happy.
Vindicated. A sure sign the
damage was remediated.

We eloped. I got married
barefoot on the beach,
with witnesses. No family attended.

My mother threw us a cocktail party
a month later. She insisted that we
register; her family and friends
wanted to buy us gifts.

"Ma," I said. "I don't live in a rabbit hutch.
We each have our own place.
We have sheets. We eat off of plates."

"All the world loves a lover!" she sang.

But your family hates me, I thought.
They would step over me down on the ground
to make it to the movies on time.

My mother spent the weeks between the
wedding and the party in the hospital. She
checked out early to meet with the caterer.

We registered at every store she suggested
and sent thank you notes promptly,
without being asked.

March 2004

The last time my daughter and I visited
my mother, we didn't know it would be
the last time. My daughter was four.
We decided to stay over, since I've never
liked driving at night. We made up nests of
foam pads and sleeping bags in the drive-in
guest closet.

After the home health aide tucked my mother
into her tidy bed, we joined her. I got out a book
I had brought: *Millions of Cats*. It's one of the only books
I remember having read to me as a child. She told me
her mother had read it to her.

My daughter snuggled between us.
We chanted the chorus:
> *Hundreds of cats,*
> *Thousands of cats,*
> *Millions and Billions and Trillions of cats!*

My mother had one hand to her
mouth. Her eyes were full. The other hand
reached out tentatively to stroke the book.
It was really there.

April 2004

By the end, before she died,
my mother forgave them all.

Except for my father.
She hated him.

Her parents, her cousins, their friends,
Dr. K. and his wife, all of them visited
her condo, borrowed best-selling books,
and watched cable movies
on her TV in the den. They all admired
photos of my daughter, the only grandchild
in the east.

Hundreds of people attended her funeral.
Dozens delivered eulogies
lauding her grace and her courage.

Except for my father.
He remained dead.

Also April 2004

My mother's children
were not so quick to forgive.
We gathered at her condo
before the memorial service,
going over the lists of people
who had been notified, or
called, or sent food, wondering
who would show up.

"X won't show," said one brother.
"Already called for time and directions," I said.

"Surely not Y," said the other brother.
"They were here for dinner three weeks ago," I said.

We went through her old address book, asking
only one question, over and over:
What did they know
and when did they know it?

April 2005

After my mother died
I was diagnosed with stage 0
breast cancer. The doctors
recommended tamoxifen.

I was leery. I asked the
hospital librarian for a
literature search.

As I was leaving Baystate
Medical Center, I saw my mother
in her scooter, with her post-
chemo gray hair, shaking her head
no, no, no.

Then I remembered she was dead
and she was gone.

I refused tamoxifen.
I told them I decided based on
reviewing the research.

Thanks, ma.

April 2007

Turns out marrying the anti-father
was also not the right answer.

I had married a man with perspective, who remarked
as an ambulance passed: Somebody's life
just got changed.

I had married a man addicted to drugs, who stole from me
and said money didn't matter, that I knew nothing
about being a family.

When our condo burned down, he made it clear
he didn't light the match.

While I was getting divorced
my mother's friend and her sister
were my supporting elders.

"My mother wouldn't approve," I said.
"She considered divorce a demerit."

"Nonsense," said her friend.
"Your mother wants that man gone."

"Nonsense," said my aunt.
"Your mother is standing with you."

Two nights later as I was getting ready
for bed, I noticed some papers on his dresser.
They were the receipts for checks he had
forged in my name. I had spent an entire
weekend searching for those check stubs.
I called anyone I thought could help me locate
or recreate them. I wanted tangible proof.

To this day I have no earthly idea
where those chits came from.

I sent them to my lawyer, attached to an affidavit.

Thanks, ma.

Recycling the Travel section

My family always read the newspaper.
When we sat for dinner—6:30 every
weeknight—you better know your news.
Sunday papers were a special treat.

For years after the secret was spilled
my mother separated the Travel section
from the Boston Sunday Globe and sent it
unread to recycling. If she had known, she said,
she would have traveled. With her children.
My mother loved London and always
wanted to return. You can't get that back.

And all that time estranged
from her children, fighting her own
decline. Some things can't be fixed.
Splintery shards remain, like the glasses
that slipped from her numb hands onto
cold hard floor.

Ma, if you're still listening: I have taken
my daughter to the ends of the earth.
California. London. Aruba. India. We saw
sunrise at the Taj Mahal. We have hiked
in the Amazon rainforest, and on top
of the Great Wall of China.

Ma, if you still care: I carry a piece of your
jewelry with us, wherever we go.

And in the end…

…the love you take is equal to the love you make.
—Lennon–McCartney, The End, 1969

Many years later, I saw on a website
that my grandfather's firm was sponsoring
my local women's shelter. I emailed my
father's friend, RM. He must be spinning,
I joked.

Your grandfather believed in pro bono, wrote
the lawyer, and in giving back.

Did not know that, I replied.

Every year they give out a judicial award
in his name, wrote the lawyer.

Did not know that, I replied.

And so in 2010 I went as a guest of the firm
to the Boston Bar Association award reception.
Afterwards we went to the Parker House for dinner.
My daughter wanted me to bring her a
Boston cream pie.

"So," said the lawyer. "You have a pre-teen.
I wish your mother could see this. What's
it like, being on the other side? You put your
parents through hell."

I stared at him. "That was a long time ago," I said.

"Did you ever talk about it?" he asked. "Did you ever
apologize to your mother?"

I reached for some water. "No," I said. "Once the secret
came out, we never looked back. We had
other priorities."

"Oh that," said his wife. "That didn't go on for very long."

I stared at her. "About 15 years," I said. "Eight of them
after my father died."

The lawyer stared at an empty chair. "I remember
the day your father came into my office," he said.
"He was a broken man. Your mother was his life.
He didn't know what to do."

"Anyway," said his wife, "there was no treatment then,
so it didn't matter. It wouldn't have made any difference."

I realized they knew the secret
but not the story.
I was their guest.
I was my mother's daughter.
I spoke slowly and gently.

"You can tell yourselves whatever you need to,"
I said. "But know this: you were part of a pact
that violated the do-no-harm clause. And all of us
were changed."

We sat in silence for a few minutes, and then
talked about headlines in the news. I ordered dessert
to go.

The Road of Life

There's more than one way home
Ain't no right way, ain't no wrong
Whatever road you might be on
Find your own way, 'cause there's more
than one way home
— Keb Mo, *More Than One Way Home*

Goodbye Dogwood Tree

When I was a little girl
I had my own bedroom,
with a dormer window.
And eaves. My little bed
was tucked under the eaves.

                      Our house
had a backyard where we could play:
a rusty swing set, a worn-to-dirt
stretch for playing catch or practicing
at bat, a small thrilling hill
for sledding. In the fall we raked leaves
and jumped in the pile before
setting them on fire. In the spring
we sought the first green moss, the
first yellow forsythia.

                    Outside my window
was a dogwood tree that threw out
glorious pink blossoms every spring.
I loved that tree. I remember once
my brother's best friend Peter
climbed out of my window and
stood on the slanted roof to get a toy
out of the tree. My mother was
horrified, but no one could stay mad
at Peter. Peter is

                  all grown up now:
he is a social worker, specializing in
gerontology, which is interesting because
both of his parents died young. The last time
I saw Peter, we took a break from
sitting shiva and took a walk

(somewhere someone is always sitting shiva,
                    and all walks end up in our old neighborhood)
Peter told me he was a step- mom; this was
decades before his marriage could be
legal because love is love is love. In the
old days, in the old neighborhood, our parents
would have been ashamed of a gay
offspring; would have kept this secret, would
have been talked about behind the sheer curtains
in other living rooms. But then came AIDS.
And no suburban mother in America
could withstand this encroaching
emaciating plague. Not killing their
neighbors' kids, the kids who had played
in everyone's yards, had doused each other
with hoses and buckets on hot days,
shared cocoa in the cold. And now
the mothers reached out. I hope your boy
is OK, they said on the phone, in busy kitchens,
between hands of bridge. Please tell me your boy
is OK.

                    It's been years
since I've heard about Peter. Now that we have
no shared elders I may never see him
again; we kids have scattered all
across the continent.

Goodbye dogwood tree.
Goodbye Peter.
Goodbye feeling firmly settled
in a carefully delineated space.

Goodbye Besties

As a little kid I always had
one special friend: first Debbie
and then Eva and then Janet and then
Elizabeth. I don't remember the transitions
but they must have been hard and dramatic
because I spent so many afternoons and
weekends and sleepovers with the
same friend. We went to each other's
family events and knew grandparents and
cousins, family quarrels and
secrets. The walls were more
porous then.

Debbie was
two years older than me, so eventually
it was no longer cool to act out books
or go wading in the pond or chasing
bottles in the creek. She got older friends.

Eva was my age
and taught me how to talk in class and
pass notes without getting caught. She got
hit by a car, out walking with her father,
and died on the spot. I didn't know how to feel
when my parents told me, I didn't know death
could take American children, my age, or that
fathers could be helpless to stop it. Later I got
very sad. I visited her parents but after a while
we ran out of things to say.

Janet got a new best friend
who liked to ride horses.

Elizabeth was my
next- door neighbor and I practically moved in
with her family. Which was great for me, but
her mother was not pleased. Then her whole
family moved to New York City.

Goodbye best friends. Goodbye
trying on and taking off
other people's families

Nightmare House

When I was in first or second grade
my family moved. Just up the street, to a
bigger house with a smaller yard. We were not
allowed to play on this lawn. Landscapers
kept the grass tended and the rhododendron
in bloom. For the new house, my parents

hired a decorator to set up each room.
There was nothing personal in any visible
space: even the silhouette profiles framed
on the wall were staged from a store. Anger
spun suspended in the dry dry air like
dust motes prohibited from landing. We kids
walked on runners to protect the carpet and
weren't allowed in the living room or dining room
unless it was a special event and we were
carefully costumed. My mother would
take us aside, and whisper/hiss:
"This is a command performance.
Watch your fucking mouths."

I had a recurring nightmare in this house.
Some details varied but there was always fire
and an invading army looking like the green
plastic soldiers my brothers had discarded.
The staircase swirled like an Escher print and
sometimes one of my brothers was hung
from the center beam. I hid within a bend
of the stairs, sometimes with the other
brother; sometimes I lost him too.
I always woke up
before I knew
if I had
escaped.

Goodbye Grade School

In the olden days we would
line up outside the locked doors every morning
before the school day began. Most of us
walked to school and sometimes envied
the kids who got a ride, although out loud
we called them sissies and spoiled.
We lined up to enter our classrooms
in order, by height. I was
second to shortest almost
every year. We sat in rows
in alphabetical order. I was
second to last, almost
every year.

There were rules.
There was order.

There was a strict dress code
especially for girls. We could only
wear pants if it was below freezing,
and then only outside. In class it was
always a dress or a skirt. The hem had to
touch the ground if you were kneeling,
as if to play jacks. We played jacks
and four-square on the blacktop at
recess and at lunch. The boys got to
run around the playground and climb
on the jungle gym. Because boys will be
boys, but we were young ladies.

There were rules.
But the order was cracking.

By the time I was in fourth grade
we stopped walking home for lunch
and ate in the classrooms or the gym.

By the time I was in fifth grade
girls could wear nice trousers or dress pants
but not blue jeans.

In sixth grade we had a record player in
the classroom and we could stay inside
for lunch. The boys went outside with a
bucket of balls and played sports. The girls
hung in the room with the music and
danced. We played "Born to be Wild"
by Steppenwolf, over and over and
over. It was our favorite song
to dance and vamp and
scream out loud. It was
so much fun. It was
the last time I remember
dancing in public
wild and free.

Yes Sir

yes sir we said yes
sir whenever he was angry,
my father, he would start in with
"listen, my friend" and we knew whatever
he said next the answer was "yes, sir" and
maybe just maybe you could escape but
today he is inflamed, he is flushed, he is
quivering mad and we scramble to get out of
his way as he storms over to the closet and
finds an old flag, from where we don't know-
maybe his father's grave- and he
sticks it on a pole, rams it into the front yard,
grabs my brother's trumpet and tries
to play taps, to play reveille, the world
has gone reeling mad, the neighbors all know and
pretend not to see: he is marching us now
yes sir around the yard racing and
screaming yes sir the flag snapping at
the corners, the corners they fold down
smooth in a tight triangle and salute
when they strip the flag from his
coffin to present to my mother, but she
steps back, so they pass it to me, but
I don't know what to do so
I stand straight and respond
yes, sir.

The Minister's Wife

She stared at me intently
through the slightly swollen eye
she swore that she had gotten by
falling down the stairs.
I never saw her take
a single clumsy step
but every time I left the house
she had a silly accident
and wore another bruise.
Listen up, she insisted.
This is truly something
you can always count on.
There are three parts water
to one part concentrate
in each and every pitcher
of frozen orange juice.
That's the American way.

Borderlines

Sometimes I walked all night and slept at school during the day, under a table, behind the blinds, beside the beds in the boarding boys' dorm. I wasn't at Kent State but I was wounded; I wasn't at the Watergate but eavesdropping devices were trying to steal my secrets while murmuring lies. I was not a crook. I was born the same year as that girl running down the road in Vietnam, naked, limbs akimbo, burning from the napalm, fleeing from the fire. Sometimes my skin sloughed off in sheets.

Nights I was too tired to walk I hid between the prickly ornamental bushes and the stolid foundations of suburban homes. I sang Blowing in the Wind, I sang Long Black Veil, softly, over and over, waiting for the sun, for safe passage. I found snakes in the landscaping, waddling skunks, broken- necked bodies of birds that had crashed into clean clear windows. I sang Amazing Grace when I buried the birds. I forgot how to pray, I forgot how to cry, I forgot to be scared of tests given at school, I forgot nice ladies wore gloves into town, I forgot there was a better day coming. I kept on keeping on. I shut my eyes but still I saw; I hid screaming but made no sound. I survived.

I survived. I bend, I blend: I am your neighbor, I am your friend. I feed your kids cut fruit and chocolate milk; I rinse dishes in a double sink. I keep a tidy, orderly house. Screens shield the windows. Sometimes my mind spins and scenery sways but I hold my head high: nobody knows where I've been. At night I lock up tight. I am on the inside, in the warmth, in the dry; indeed, I survived.

Free Range

The summer after junior high
a friend and I packed up a backpack
and a 6-string acoustic guitar.
We wandered the beaches of Cape Cod
and the Islands for about six weeks.

Sometimes we stayed with friends
or friends of friends, or extended family
on vacation. Sometimes we took out
our guitar and sang folk songs on the
village green or the steps of a church
until someone invited us home.

One night my friend's parents
met up with us, stayed with us for
a night or two in a hotel, and then
drove us to our next destination.

One night my parents
met up with us, took us to a nice
dinner with many Vodka Collins,
and then drove away, leaving us
drunk and alone
in the parking lot. What the hell
just happened? asked my friend.
I shrugged. We stuck out our thumbs
and sang Mercedes Benz
over and over
until somebody
picked us up.

We spent two nights
on Nantucket, at the summer cottage of one of
my father's clients, married to my mother's
childhood rival. The wife was going blind. The
husband worked late, missed the ferry, never
joined us. The wife played a wicked blues
harmonica. We drank several silver pitchers
of Scotch Sours.

A couple of nights
we slept out on the beach. I'll always remember
waking up at ebb tide at
sunrise. We spent hours
creating an elaborate mural, scraping
the sand with sharp sticks, embellishing
with shells and rocks, sea glass and
driftwood. We then spent hours
watching our vision slowly
swallowed, smoothed over
by the rising tide.

Goodbye My First Love

I didn't have a lot of friends
sophomore year. New school.
My same old life. The academic
calendar had seven separate terms
of 4½ weeks each. It was
Alternative. Experimental.
Disruptive. I skipped one entire term
and worked on a self-sufficient farm
getting back to the land, to
set my soul free. When I went
back to school, you threw a jacket
near my chair and said,
"Welcome back." You noticed
I had been gone.
That was the start.

We dated but not
exclusively. I was still a virgin
and your other girlfriends were not.
Still we had a connection. A couple of nights
when I had no place to stay I snuck into a barn
on your parent's property. A couple of nights when
my foster parents were acting weird you snuck in my
window. One afternoon when my parents were out of the
country you stole my father's car and we dropped acid. We
visited friends, hiked at the reservoir, and then you dropped me
at the multi-service center for my group therapy session. I was
so very proud
I made it on the right day
at the right time.

We were such
a winning team.

Then you decided to spend the night
with the only girl in the world
I asked you to stay away from: my
beach buddy. You took her virginity.
I had painted a target
you couldn't resist.

I broke up with
both of them.

Revelation

If I were to tell you what I see, would you love me still?
—Janet Longe Sadler

Here in the pale green hallways
a skeleton is staring, drugged eyes
sunk in bony sockets; he tried to
starve himself, wasted away to
frailty and chills; now he munches
rye toast, walking slowly on skinny
white legs, leaving a trail of
dry crumbs; walks passed the jew who
decided one night that he was
the true jesus; who walked out
barefoot through the snow,
proclaiming his message and all
that was divine; who was carried in
raving and now sits rocking, rocking,
rocking, cradling feet swathed in
white bandages, blackened
frostbitten skin, nearly lost
toes; he believes the doctors
down in the ER drained all of his
powers, all of his sacred love;
he seeks his debrided skin as if
the shredded scales are holy, as if
we could still be saved.

Night clouds.

The sky is out tonight.
I clench my hands into fists
to fight the chill, and ward off
any attempt to count time
on my fingers.
I open my eyes fiercely
refusing to see
pages from a calendar
soaking up the rich red blood
of my imagination.
Seven months have passed
since my child wasn't born.
Stubbornly I cling
to the list of rationales
that supported me then
as now. And why not
believe?
Still I sometimes shiver
to see a candle
snuffed.
One flick of the wrist
and the flame
is over.

to Norman

You came from an ancient reservation:
a painted mesa surrounded by
sacred spirits. As a child
you learned grandmother's stories,
watched dancers down from the mountains
etched into the night by the flickering fire
   shadows leap and writhe still
      in the black depths of your eyes-
Sometimes after the ceremonies
the police took your father away
drunk. Other times they didn't
and you lay listening to the rhythm
of the thumps and grunts as he
beat your mother. Now you sit
amidst the clamor and fire-engine wails
of downtown Phoenix. My mission
is to convince you that 2 pints
equals 1 quart
and drill for multiplication tables.

Character Study #1

The older daughter, Nora,
had dark hair, dark eyes,
an impish look, almond brown skin.
I say older but she was maybe 4,
not in school, always dancing or
jiggling or making up songs or
hanging on her mother, who was
always frustrated with her. Just go
do something! her mother would say.
Now! Somewhere else! Nora
always hovered, always
at the edge, never at rest.
The younger daughter

Bernie had fair hair, a
chubby toddler tummy,
and a hare lip. They had started
treatment for her palate but still
when she spoke, no one but her mother
or Nora understood. Her mother's boyfriend,
Ron, used to say: Bernie speaks Russian.
Ron had fair hair and the start of a
beer gut but they said Ron was
not the father. Both girls,
dark and fair,

were from Deb's first husband,
Carl. Carl was older and walked painfully
on two canes. I knew this because
we stayed overnight at his house,
while the girls visited. There was a
fountain in the courtyard and we slept in one room

with bunkbeds. I was in my early twenties,
our boyfriends worked at the same place,
we had no boundaries and odd events
happened all the time.

Deb told me it was a bad marriage.
Carl was cruel, abusive; when she had
Bernie she was afraid to leave
Nora in his care. For a few months
Nora had a foster family. And again,
during the divorce, or maybe
they were together in a shelter,
it was never clear. I don't remember
when Deb and her girls met Ron.
It was before I drove west, ending up
with my boyfriend in Arizona (odd events
happen all the time). Mostly Deb told me

Ron was a nice guy, the best. He didn't
let her have a car- where did she
need to go, with two little kids?
But they rarely fought. Deb was
happy to be at home. Life wasn't
always this good, she told me,
one afternoon, after I had driven her
to run errands. We sat drinking beer
while the girls played in a shallow
Walmart wading pool. Deb told me
about being fourteen and fighting with
her own mom, constantly,
fiercely. Deb's mom grew up
on the reservation and threatened
to send Deb back home, to learn

the old ways. Deb ran away with a friend,
then met a guy, the friend went home,
and Deb ended up
turning tricks, somehow in Hawaii. One day
she was sitting on a dirty bedspread,
staring, stoned, not caring anymore,
and a guy came into her room. She assumed
it was her next John but it was her step dad,
come to take her home. She didn't look at faces
then. Odd things happen all the time.

Ron's such a nice guy, Deb told me. But still.
Sometimes they fought, the kids got on his nerves,
especially Nora, always *always* in the way.
So Deb had a plan. She put saccharine tablets
in her monthly pill packets.
She flushed the pills. She figured
she'd be pregnant soon. And then
Ron couldn't leave—then
he would stay forever.

I drank a little more. Even in my early twenties
I knew this was a bad plan. I played horseshoes
with Nora. I asked if she was excited
to start school. Yes! she said,
looking at her mom. Later Nora asked
if I knew where school was, and if she would
have to go away. I told her I'd find her school
and maybe we could drive over
with mom and Bernie and visit.
Nora liked that plan. I don't remember
if we ever did it.

I moved home to New England,
without the boyfriend. I grew up.
I don't know what happened to that
family. I carried a picture of the four of them
in my wallet for years, a family portrait
from Sears. Deb and Ron were smiling straight
into the camera. Bernie was looking down
at a stuffed dog in her lap. Nora, for once
not in motion, was looking up at her
mother, making sure she was still there
after the flash was gone.

Goodbye Marriage

We accept the love we think we deserve.
—Stephen Chbosky, *The Perks of Being a Wallflower*

I liked living alone. When I had
my own place, there was one safe spot
on the whole vast planet
where I was always welcome and
capable and Queen of the World.

                    But still
for some reason
I gave all that up
to be what my mother
always wanted me to
be: Married. To a man.

                    We moved in together
and so we met (finally)
all of those expectations.
From the outside
it looked alright. I had
a job and a husband and even
a yellow dog. From the inside
it was a lie. Oh the dog was golden,
well-behaved and charming,
and I brought home a steady
paycheck, to cover rent and
insurance and buy food.
But my husband

                    was an addict.

I thought I was cool enough and
tough enough and independent
enough to pull it all off.
I wasn't.

                              Living with an addict
is hell. Living with an addict
who convinces you that you
are the problem, that fussing
over money could kill any
couple, that family was bigger
than that; who makes you afraid
to speak your truth, to make him
angry, because to make him feel
bad costs $120 and the baby is
hungry and you need to pay
daycare; living with a partner
who steals from you and lies
to your face; life with an addict
is an inner circle of hell
littered with thousands
of sins.

                              And through it all
you become smaller and smaller
and more and more alone, as the
lies grow stickier, larger and larger
because you have to be loyal to your
husband, or else
why be married?
Why,
indeed?

In the end
I remember pacing on the phone
tight concentric circles inside a parking lot
behind the mill that was my office.
"You need to take responsibility
for your actions," I said. "I don't
even know what that means,"
he replied. "I know," I said.
"That's the problem."

My next call
was to a lawyer
(finally).

Mourning the Living

It's harder to mourn for the living than the dead.
    I'm ashamed to say that out loud.
        My mama would slap my face and
            spit three times. But it's true.

My ex- has been an addict for a hundred years.
    Sometimes he says he's done—can't stand
        any more damage—but wait a day, a week,
            and he's using again. Mama should slap *his* face.

Our daughter used to believe him because
    that's what kids do. Now she knows better.
        It hurts to look in her eyes and see
            love bleeding out. But it's true.

Her dad has been an addict for a hundred years.
    Damage done is done. Even Jesus wept.
        I make her snack and shake my head.
            It's harder to mourn for the living than the dead.

Goodbye Ben

There's a tear in the world:
Ben has flown free.
He put down a bottle;
he picked up a gun. In that flash
it was finished. There are no
take-backs. There is no
next level. For Ben,
there is no more pain.
There's a Ben- shaped
tear in the world:
We are all left behind.

And we sob. We can't believe
and then we can't think of
anything else. We can't eat
                we eat junk.
We can't sleep
                we nap through class.
We cling to each other
                we all die alone.
We forget why we walked
into a room. We vow to never forget
sweet, awkward Ben.
There's a tear in the world:
Ben has flown free.
We are all left behind.

Trauma teachers tell us
it will get better, with time.
                Ben is outside of time
We will find a new normal.
            we will never
         feel normal
      again.

We mingle in the churchyard
surrounded by sturdy orange pumpkins.
     I want to smash the smug pumpkins.
 We tell stories, of the bright boy who knew
all of the presidents, vice-presidents, and major achievements
of each administration
               dude could kill a bottle of vodka in 2 days.
of the good friend who always listened and
brought bags of candy.
             dude did you see the slices all up his arms?
Did the police talk to you? Was he bullied?
        dude remember when he made a Facebook
        as Eric Harris?
He was so talented, on the computer, with his videos.
        dude did you know he made Columbine
        mashups? dubbed over the security footage
        with soundtrack and screams, it was raw—
        dude it was totally sick—

Why didn't anyone see any signs? Wasn't there anything
we could have done?

We file into pews, to pray, to sing hymns, surrounded by
pictures of Ben with family and friends, with his
date to the homecoming dance
(my daughter). When six 15 year old boys
rise as young men to carry the coffin
through tears I see how their faces will be set
years from now, when their parents pass,
or their wives leave, or
(God forbid) they bury a child.
All the losses of their lives
will now be measured
in magnitudes of Ben.

It's the 10th anniversary

of my divorce. I'm on a flight, half-way
back from Aruba, writing in my journal:
planning the marketing for my book,
making a grocery list for
my daughter's graduation party.
I won't think about work until tomorrow.

My daughter is in the seat beside
mine, slowly reading page after page of
handwritten letters, pencil scrawled on
yellow paper, from her father in the
Essex County Jail. Detox is going well.
He likes the program, and his cellmate;
he quotes the Bible, says his reading glasses
are almost broken, but all his money
goes for cigarettes.

In Aruba we saw leatherback turtle nests
all along Eagle Beach. The female turtle returns
to the same shore where she was born, hauls herself
laboriously up the beach, laying dozens of eggs in a
single nest, flippers flinging fine sand. Then
she returns to the sea. Sixty to seventy days later,
the hatchlings must fend for themselves,
making their way to the water at dusk,
alone. We watched one night as the
last baby turtle reached the Caribbean, got
tossed back by a wave, and crawled forward
again. The ranger said we're not allowed
to interfere. Tears were streaming down my face.
We walked to the closest restaurant, ordered two
fruity drinks, spiked with dark rum.

Grateful for Good Neighbors

for Tom and Marge Crosby

Thank you, kind sir. You saw
something not right—a child?
a doll? —tossed awkwardly in a
pile of leaves. But what's important

is this: you stopped. You went back.
Out of your way, late for work,
you listened to that little voice—
something is not right—and you found

a small girl. A toddler, naked and weary,
burned and bruised—tortured—alone—
in that pile of wet leaves. And you and your wife,
you gathered that child up, in your

arms, in your coat, and you brought that
baby home. Thank you. In a crazy mad world
we are told to look for the helpers. And you,
you two, on that morning, by that act,

you saved a small girl, and also
a tattered shred of my soul.

The Busboy from the Ambassador Hotel

I held history in my hands
and it bled out. I don't know why.
I was nobody then. The bullet
that missed me took his life
and shattered my country. Why
he stopped to shake my hand,
a Mexican busboy spattered with
grill grease, I will never know.
He fell before I even heard the gun.
I held his head up off the hard floor,
I didn't want him to be alone, to die
for me. He wasn't Jesus. I grabbed
rosary beads from my pocket and
placed them in his splayed palm.
I prayed. I changed the course of the world
by taking his hand. The photographer
changed the course of my life
with that one haunted shot.
If only we could do it
all over again, I would step
into the path
of the bullet.

Off the Trail

Remembering Gerry Largay

When you find my body
please call my daughter. Tell her
her mama will be with her
always. Steady as the sun.

When you find my body
look for my car. There's a
jacket in there, snacks,
a map. I must have gotten lost.

When you find my body
breathe. Look at what you see.
Listen to the human noise
in the space between heartbeats;

feel the atoms warmed by the sun
or cooled in its absence. Maybe
there are others with you. Maybe
it is you alone in the woods.

When you find my body
I will no longer be cold or hungry.
Please, call my daughter.
Then, save yourself.

Germanwings 9525

24 March 2015

It was a mild mid- morning in March
when the plane, after a short delay, took off
from Barcelona. There were 56 empty
seats; there were 144 passengers
on board; there were 6 crew members.
There were no survivors.

There were 16 German high school students
heading home that Tuesday. Sixteen lives on the cusp,
aborted. The girl in row 16 sobbed,
wished she had kissed that boy who stared at her,
wished she had hugged her mother and not
turned away, not refused to let her mother help
pack and carry her bag. Iche liebe meine
mutter, she says, over and over, her stomach in her
ears, her ears throbbing, now she is screaming,
I love my mother.

The pilot knocks at the
locked cockpit door.
The copilot breathes steadily
in silence.

The baby in row 11 wails.
His ears hurt, thinks the mama.
She starts to shush and rock her child.
The papa points out the window
with a shaking hand. Look.
Now the mama rocks and prays,
singing the lullaby her mama sang to her:
Sleep, baby, sleep.
Sleep, baby, sleep.

She calls on all of the angels of God
to spare her only child.
If this impossible thing is happening
maybe a miracle is possible too.

The businessman in seat 3A gives up
doodling on his expense report
and cries for the child that
he won't see grow up; for the wife
he won't kiss again; for ever leaving home
for a stupid business trip. The businessman thanks God
for life insurance, hopes that his wife never finds
those pictures tucked up and zipped into
his briefcase pocket: Please, God,
spare her that. And mama,
meine gelibte mutter,
I love you.

The pilot backs up,
lunges at the unrelenting door.
The copilot breathes steadily
in silence.

The retired grandma in row 22
closes her eyes
thanks heaven for this last week
with the children
and their children, precious
kindele; she wings a prayer
to her best friend through all these
last long years; remembers
being fond of her husband,

and prepares to meet him
and her blessed mother
when the plane plunges
into the blanket of snow
spread over the rugged mountains.

The bass baritone in row 9,
whose honeyed low notes
resonated with dramatic emotion,
is reduced to sobbing and calling out
for Ave Maria,
Mother of God.

The pilot shouts orders and codes,
thrashing at the door.
The copilot breathes steadily
in silence.

The stewardesses hug each other.
They know crash position
won't do a damn thing.
They think of the hours spent
trying to identify the enemy in the crowd
while all along evil
was standing beside them,
in uniform. And this is how
it will end.

The high school boy in row 17
is sorry that insisting on sex
ever made Annika cry;
hopes his father remembers
how proud he was
when he made that basket at the buzzer,

and when he stood up to those
jerks at the park, even though
the kid they were picking on
really was a dork.

The pilot steadies himself
pictures his mother, young and
tender and sleepy, tucking him
back into bed. He apologizes for
his hubris. The pilot, bellowing,
tries to overthrow fate
but he can't.

The baby in row 33 puts her hands
to her ears and shrieks. Her mama
screams too, counting her rosaries
on baby's flexed toes,
begging forgiveness
for minor forgettable sins.

The copilot, breathing steadily
in silence, disables all alarms
overrides auto-corrections
and recalibrates
his deliberate descent.

The American mother and daughter in row 27
clutch hands as the earth hurtles closer;
the mother closes her eyes, refuses to believe;
the daughter screams "What is happening?"
over and over, as if
translating into a different language could
change the certain course.

The unthinkable happens:
 the plane crashes in flames.

For days the crews search at the Ravin de Rose´,
melted snow refrozen around
chunks of char and melted metal. They find
scattered teeth and bones. They report
headaches, some nausea, some
shortness of breath. Possibly
high altitude sickness; the plane
hit the mountain at 5,000 feet. Possibly
the sudden release of 150 souls
returned to stardust and ash.
At night the inspector from the local village
goes home, scrubs away the grit and
warms his hands; climbs into bed
giving thanks for his home and family,
for the mother who loved him and the father
who raised him to be the kind of man
who walks into the wreckage of hell and
tries to mend it, or at least
comprehend. He prays for a dreamless sleep,
but awakens again and again
to the phantom cries
of the anguished pilot
banging
on the cockpit door.

The reporter on the spot
once so jaded and cynical
always good for another round of drinks
sets aside his cell phone

ceasing to follow and retweet;
turns off the TV with captions
the radio with constant commentary,
and closing his tired eyes, thinks back
to the last time he told his mother
he loved her; the last time
he saluted his father, lost in
old stories of a forgotten, predictable
war. The reporter is haunted
by the madness of the copilot
breathing steadily, in silence,
for the 10 long minutes
he dove towards destruction.
The restless reporter
feels his lips moving in prayer
for the eternal salvation
of the pilot
blocked
by the locked cockpit door.

Every Addict is Somebody's Child

I made sure my daughter died with good credit and no police record.
Imagine that.
—The Heroin Crisis, Newburyport News 12/21/15

I

Grandma's pills are gone
again, and my wife's bracelet
from our 15th anniversary, it's
missing, and the fifty dollars
stashed in my toolkit
isn't there. What the hell.
If anything is broken,
daddy will fix it. But
deep deep inside
there's a hole
in her soul.

I get so angry. I yell and threaten
and tell her I'm done—
I've gone as far as I can go—
but then look at her and know
I will love and protect my child
for the rest of my life. So
I convince the cop she's a good kid
who got sleepy after curfew;
I drag her butt out of bed to the therapist
and to meetings and the unemployment office
when she loses her job. Again.
When she tells me
the lights are going out, daddy,
first I freeze and then
I pay the electric. I tell her
she needs to be more responsible
but she crumbles, crying, she has

disappointed me—again—
and she feels so bad, so bad.
So I hold her and tell her I love her,
but even while I'm hugging her I know
she's going out to use again
to smother this fresh pain.
Because deep down inside
there's a hole
in her soul.

II

I was down in my work room
making something, making a mess,
thinking about how we got here
and what is wrong with that kid
and how do I fix this, how do I fix her—
  is this a disease
    or is that an excuse—
when there was a knock on the door.
And even though I told her a hundred times
this was going to happen—told her
some day she would wake up dead—
until the man in uniform said they
couldn't revive her, I never came close
to imagining how much it hurts.
So bad. My baby is
gone. All of my life
up until that day—
gone. When she died,
everything stopped:

when she died,
something
dropped.
Deep down inside,
there's a hole
in my soul.

Dangerous Women

It was her first concert
out with friends. The gang of girls.
Besties since babies, they said.
They picked outfits and did their hair,
one high ponytail, smoky eyes. They listened
to their parents lecture and promised
to follow the signs and obey the rules and
not take drinks from strangers and
oh my god mom, relax. It's a concert.
Not a bar. Not a North-West Derby
brawl. Just a bunch of girls
dancing and screaming to their
favorite songs. It was Ariana Grande
live on stage: Manchester Arena
Manchester England
22 May 2017.

Three girls, who decided
at the last minute not to wear
kitten ears- three bold teens
walked into the concert as if
they owned the world.

One girl died on the floor,
shattered; the last thing she saw
bouquets of pink balloons
rising towards the ceiling.

The second girl bled from wounds
scattered about her body. She is
in hospital now, hooked up to tubes,
waiting on tests. For several hours
she asked so many questions, over
and over, but now she does not.

She answers the doctors queries,
shifts for the nurses hands: yes, her
ears are still ringing; yes, she still
smells burnt tubing. She sips water
and stares. Shell shock, they whisper.
Her ma and da take turns at her
bedside or tending the others
back home.

The third girl went home
uninjured. She spent a little
longer in the loo and got
separated from her friends.
She lost her voice
screaming for hours.
Now she won't talk, doesn't
eat, doesn't drink. She lies
curled on her bed, clutching
the string from a pink
balloon. When she goes
to the bathroom, her mum
stands by the doorway, crooning
a lullaby. They call her
uninjured, because
she didn't bleed
at the scene.

She lay in her bed while
day broke up night, again
and again. And on the third
day she called her mum.
Mum, she whispered, wide eyed,
after the bomb there was blood
on the walls, I got so scared.

I was alone! she said,
alone alone. But then
I saw a lady, almost like you,
and she stopped running to lift
up a little girl who had fell.
And the girl, she just hung
on, and I remembered to
look for the helpers.

That's right, said her mum,
stroking her hair.
Look for the helpers.

And then I was running and screaming
and in the big room, in the hotel,
there was a lady, black as pitch, she
smelled like soap, said the girl. And
I was shaking and looking all around
and she came and held me. I
don't even know who she is.

That was Amina, said her mum.
She works for the hotel, she
cleans the rooms. She left her own
country to flee the bombs and
find food. Now she lives here.
And she found you.

Mum, said the girl. I know
what I want to do now. I know.

What's that? asked her mum.
I want to be a helper, said the
girl. And she got out of bed.

Between My Fingers Like A Shield

I carry shards of glass
in my pockets. I broke the mirror.
I didn't want to see.

Pretty gets catcalled.
Pretty gets groped by anonymous hands.
Men press against Pretty's behind
on the bus. Pretty gets winks and told
to smile more. I don't
wash my hair. I don't
make up my face. My daddy
is afraid I like girls. But that's not
the worst thing.

Daddy, your friends used to
blow smoke in my face and feel up
my rear. Used to look down my shirt
while I fetched a coaster. Daddy, after a
few drinks, your friends are too friendly.
I don't wash my hands. They don't
want me touching their food anymore.
They call me a slob. But that's not
the worst thing.

The boy next door, I thought
he was my friend, Daddy. The
varsity team invited me
to a party. I was happy then.
Daddy, those boys
are not
my friends.

Daddy, Pretty is dead.
Pretty got raped. Now I just

walk around in this dirty body
try to make it through the day
untouched.

Pray for me, Daddy.
They say Jesus loves a sinner
and blesses the unwashed. I'll be
right over here
waiting for a sign
clutching shards of glass.

Sisters on the Runway

Every step. Every strut
in 5 inch stilettos
I am stomping. This
is my debut. My head
is a mile high, my smile
is shiny wide, and I. Am.
Fabulous.
        (snaps in
    Z formation)

When they first said
the fundraiser was a fashion show,
I thought it was nuts. This
is Hannah's House. A shelter,
service center, sanctuary
for women. But the others got all
giggly and giddy like kids at a
pageant. I'm a big girl. I'm
tough. But I know, at least
on the outside, I am
Ugly.

My daddy told me first.
I got a spot on my chin
and he said I was too disgusting
to sit at his table. I ate dinner
in the cellar like a dog. I made myself
small, small as I could. Hiding in corners
cuts you down.

My boyfriend said I was beautiful
when he wanted a blowjob. Otherwise
it was the other 'b' word. And he hit.
I got scars on my boobs where he

branded his initials with a lit
cigarette. No other man will want you
now they know you're mine, he said.
I took it for a while. He said
he loved me so much
it made him crazy. I took it
for too long. I left with
nothing. I was nobody
even inside my own head.

I didn't know what to do.
I married young, then moved in
with my boyfriend when my husband
left for someone younger. Never held a
real job. Didn't know how to make a
budget or pay bills. Hannah's House
helped me open my first bank account.
I'm at the head of the table now.

I'm a big girl. Curvy.
But Cathy, she called me
Voluptuous
and she said it with a wink
that made me feel delicious.
So here I am. Sass in stilettos.
I am wearing a bold, bright,
curve- lovin' gown, baby. A
push-up bra with wicked
peek-at-me lace. I. Am.
Gorgeous. Cindy did my make-up
and Maggie did my hair and when
I teared up Ruthie clapped
and said, Strike a pose!
Suddenly I was

All. That. We lined up
behind the curtain, listening
to the hoots and hollers for the
women onstage. Ruthie
asked if I was ready and I
jutted out my hip and said,
Honey, I was
born ready.

I raised my hand

and said I, too, was a poet.
We sat at small tables overlooking

The Bund, boats on the water, the red
Chinese flag flapping in the breeze. It was

lunchtime, a poetry panel at the Shanghai
International Literary Festival. The readers

were from Singapore, Mozambique,
Cambridge, Hong Kong. We discussed

history, colonization, how small towns
anywhere in the world are alike, how people

all over the earth need water, shelter, salt,
a mother tongue. At home a storm gathered

up the east coast. At home a high school boy
with a Glock shot two students and died

from his wounds. We don't know who
fired the final shot.

Touring in the People's Republic of China

March 2018

It was 5:55 and my phone battery was at 55%
when I went to watch the bustling world go by

from a bench in People's Square, Shanghai. Yesterday
we were with our guide in Beijing, at the Gate of

Heavenly Peace, where Mao Tse-Tung proclaimed the
People's Republic of China. I bought a copy of the little

red book, in English and Mandarin, and a beautiful
bookmark, painted on a leaf. At the Forbidden City we saw

craftsmanship and many fine arts, carefully preserved
for the benefit of the people. Our guide Jack was

very proud. He told us once a year the government
brings back Chinese people from around the world

for a tour, so they know what makes them Chinese.
The tour starts in the Great Hall of the People, in

Tiananmen Square. Also Jack guides groups adopting
Chinese babies, or bringing older children back

to see where they came from. Jack is from a small village
where life is slow, he says. After lunch they play mah jong

before going back to work. Life is simple there. Jack
is the oldest, his mother had three sons, but his uncle

had none, so she gave her brother the youngest of her
children. But the boy died, at ten, and the uncle was childless

again. He opened a shop and one day in the dooryard
he found a basket, and in the basket, a baby girl. The uncle

adopted the girl and she gave him three children so now
he is happy. The greatest filial obligation, gift,

duty to your family, is to have a son, to carry on
the family name. Our guide has one son, seven years

old, already he is learning English and to cook for himself,
simple meals when his parents are at work. There used to be

a one child, one family rule and it was very hard. Especially
for the farmers, they wanted more than one. But if the

government found out, there was a huge fine, a lot of
money, and they could take your house or the home

of your parents or your brother or sister. That's how
the rule was kept. It was hard. Some women had to have

the surgery. Now you can have two children, one family
and that is much better.

~

Two days ago our guide took us hiking on the Great Wall.
It was a strenuous hike, rated as difficult, with lots of hills and

stairs. The mountains were lovely, blue shadows, like an old scroll
painting, but loose pebbles and dirt slid under our feet. We paused

to rest and catch our breath and Jack told us the story of the
Lady Meng Jiang: Long ago, in the Qin dynasty, a young man

105

ran away from being conscripted to build the wall. When he was
running and hiding he go so tired and so hungry and cold

he lay down in a field to die. But he woke up in a warm bed, with
a beautiful girl, the farmer's daughter, tending him. The boy stayed

and worked on the farm and the two fell in love but
on the occasion of their wedding, in their joy,

the feast and dancing lasted three days, with all of
the villagers joining in. And then the guard learned

that the groom was not local but from away, and
they found that he had evaded his duty. So the guard

captured the groom and he went to work, finally,
building the Great Wall. The work was long and hard

and every night he went out and looked to the moon
and sang his love, and every night she did the same

until one night she had a horrible nightmare, he was
cold, so very cold. And so she left the farm to bring her

husband his warm clothes. And she found the section
of the wall where he was working, hauling stone and setting

the sticky mortar, but he had died three days before.
And she wept so hard, so many bitter tears, she cried

for so long that the wall collapsed, and underneath she found
his bones. So, she brought him to the mouth of the river to bury

106

and she sang one more time to the moon and then she died.
There is a temple there, and if you visit you can still

taste her tears. After the story we forgot our legs were tired.
My daughter asked, does everyone in China know this story?

Jack said yes, this story from the time of the dynasties is part
of being Chinese. And we walked on, to the warm dinner

awaiting us. We ate together, my daughter and I, our guide and
the driver, around a round table. The daughters of the landlady

served us, their sons kicking a soccer ball and making funny faces
for a laughing baby, all beneath a portrait of the benevolent
Chairman Mao.

Meeting the Host Family

There are smiles all around the table.
Grandma Oma nods, encouraging us all to

eat, eat. Grandpa is still in the kitchen,
still cooking. Grandma approves my

fledgling chopstick skills. I am an American
Polish Latvian Jew, visiting China, where my

Episcopalian WASP Jewish daughter is teaching
English to a 4 year old German Chinese girl, who is

proudly waving pink plastic chopsticks with
pictures of Peppa Pig, a British cartoon, and crying

"Look at me, look at me!!" while she stuffs
an entire yummy dumpling into her mouth.

Primate Customs

The nice young Vietnamese scientist
working in the park with pygmy slow loris
could not believe I was travelling solo.
No family? No one to bring with you?
He had a lovely British-accented English
and was clearly concerned.

The next day I checked into a
charming hotel on the beach, on
the South China Sea, just beyond
a fishing village. The room number
was my mother's street address.

I do not believe in coincidence.
I am not traveling alone.

About the Author

Elizabeth S. Wolf writes because telling stories is how we make sense of our world, how we heal, and how we celebrate. Elizabeth is the author of two chapbooks: the 2018 Rattle Chapbook Contest winner *Did You Know?* (Rattle, 2019) and *What I Learned: Poems* (Finishing Line Press, 2017). Elizabeth's poems have appeared in multiple anthologies and journals, including *Persian Sugar in English Tea* (in English & Farsi), *Mosaics, Ibbetson Street, Peregrine Journal, Tuck Magazine,* and others. She is a regular at the Merrimac Mic open mic and the Full Moon Story Slam. Elizabeth lives in Massachusetts and works as a metadata librarian.

www.ingramcontent.com/pod-product-compliance
Lightning Source LLC
Chambersburg PA
CBHW022156080426
42734CB00006B/459